QUESTION MARKS SAY

"WHAT?"

written by
MICHAEL DAHL

illustrated by
CHRIS GARBUTT

PICTURE WINDOW BOOKS
a capstone imprint

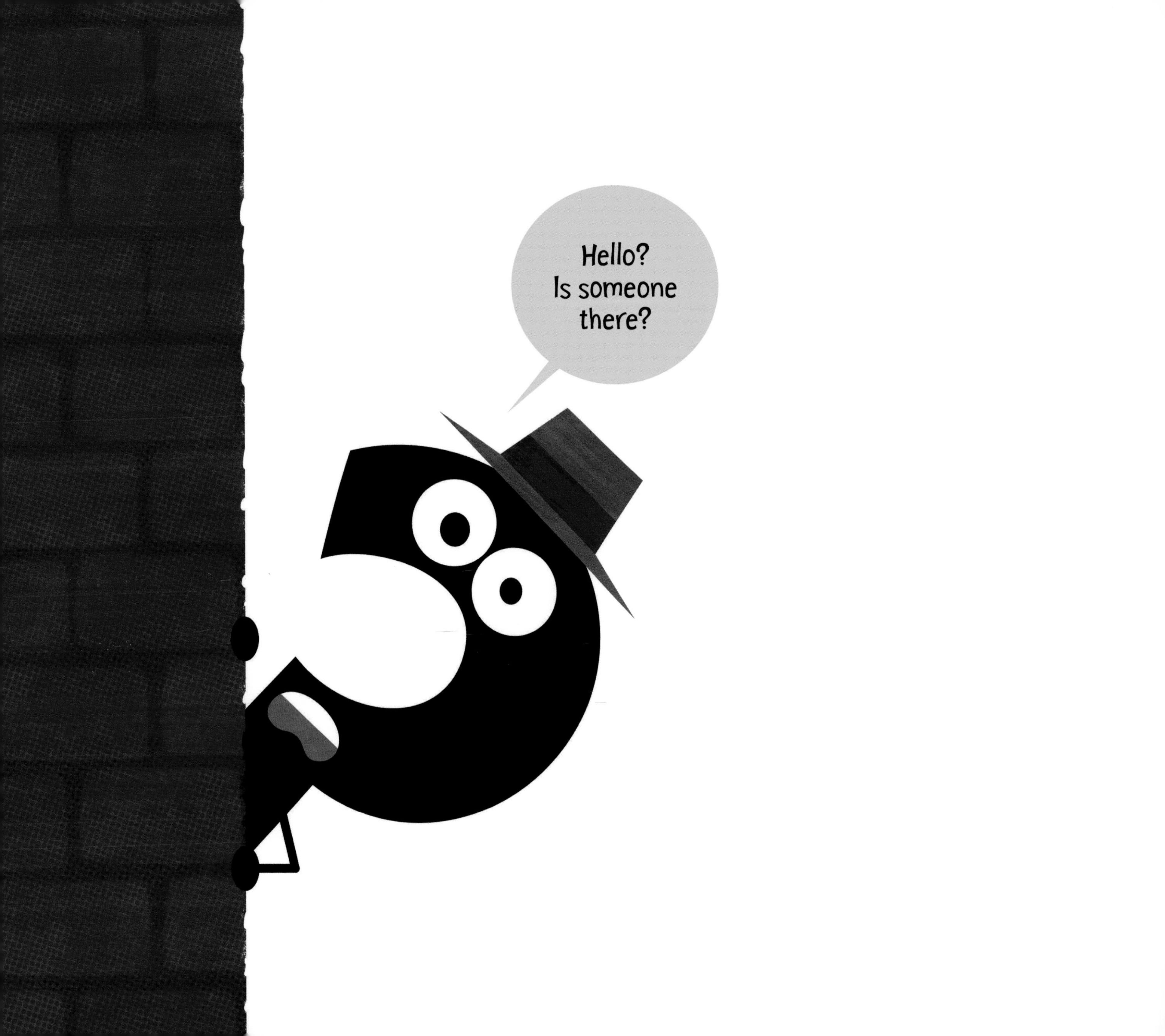
Hello? Is someone there?

Where do we find a question mark?

Questions often begin with WHO, WHAT, WHERE, WHEN, or WHY.

WHO put all of these hats here?

WHAT does this mean?

WHERE is that hot-air balloon going?

WHY are all of the hats blue?

WHEN will these questions be answered?

We ask a question when we want to know WHO.

We ask a question when we want to know WHAT.

We ask a question when we want to know WHERE.

WHERE is that hat going?

We ask a question when we want to know WHEN.

WHY is used to ask questions too.

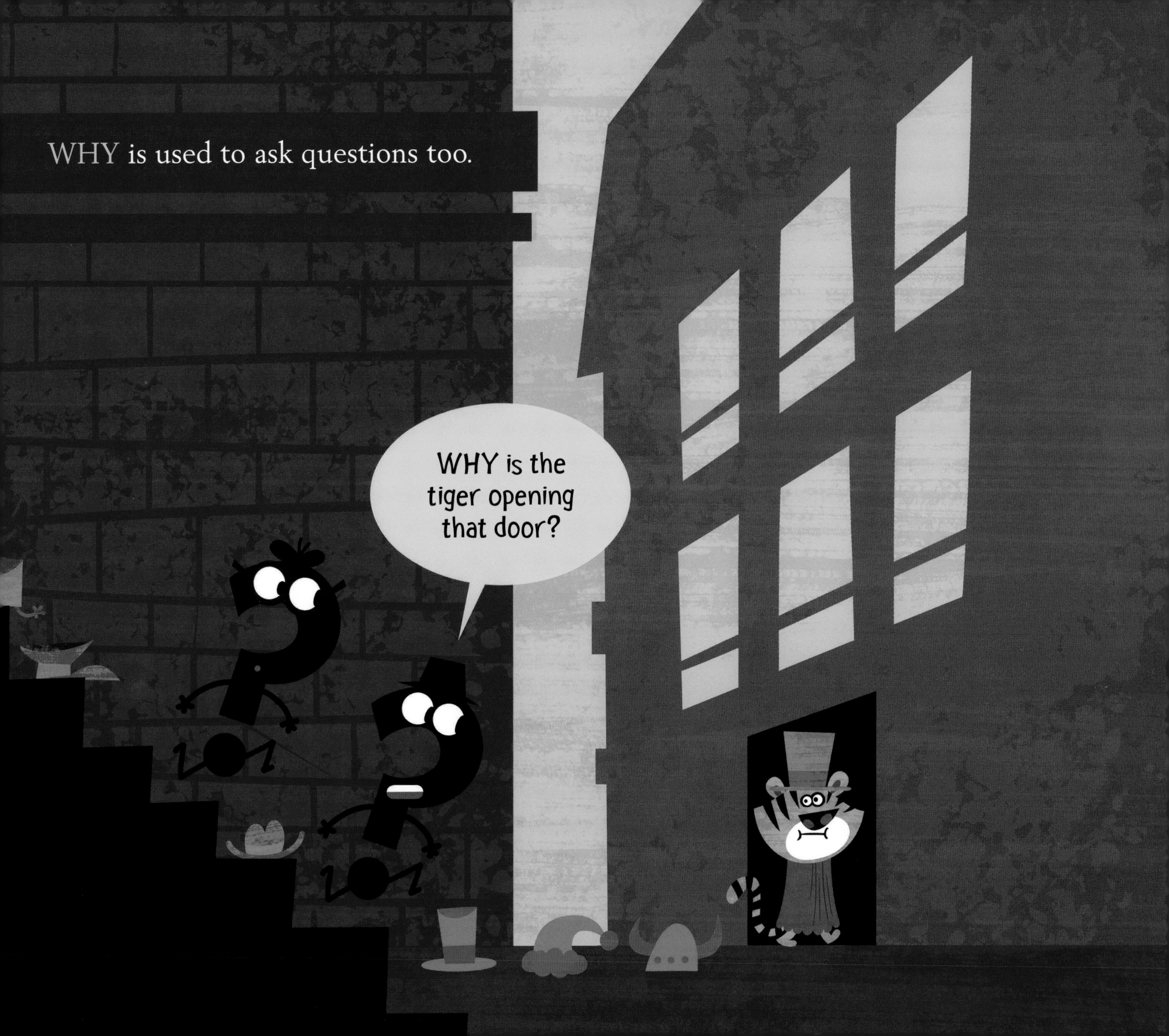

Today is Blue Hat Day!

That's WHY I had to fly the hot-air balloon. I had to find new hats to replace the ones that had blown away.

WHY did the hats blow away?

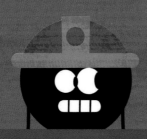

Question marks are found at the end of
SENTENCES THAT ASK QUESTIONS.

Are you enjoying this book?

Can you help us find question marks?

Question marks help us get facts. They ask WHO, WHAT, WHEN, WHERE, and WHY.

Who lost these hats?

Who is in that hot-air balloon?

What is that tiger doing?

What is behind that door?

QUESTION MARK

When will
this mystery
be solved?

When can we
go home?

Where is the
tiger going?

Where are
you going?

Why weren't
we invited to
the party?

Why does
this book have
to end?

ABOUT THE AUTHOR

Michael Dahl is the author of more than 200 books for children and has won the AEP Distinguished Achievement Award three times for his nonfiction. He is the author of the bestselling *Bedtime for Batman* and *You're A Star, Wonder Woman!* picture books. He has written dozens of books of jokes, riddles, and puns. He likes to play with words. In grade school, he read the dictionary for fun. Really. And his favorite words are adverbs (*really* is an adverb, by the way).

ABOUT THE ILLUSTRATOR

Chris Garbutt hails from a family of tea-drinking hedgehogs that live deep in the magical hills of Yorkshire in the north of England. He has spent most of his time on this planet drawing cartoons and comics in London, Paris, and most recently Los Angeles, where he now creates funny pictures in exchange for cake. Most recently he has been the executive producer, show-runner, and art director of a new TV series he co-created at Nickelodeon called *Pinky Malinky*.

GLOSSARY

case—a set of facts

crime scene—the place where something happened that was against the law

mystery—something that is hard to explain or understand

question—a sentence that asks something

replace—to take the place of

solve—to find the answer to a problem

Looking for definitions?

READ MORE

Cleary, Brian P. *The Punctuation Station*. Minneapolis: Millbrook Press, 2010.

Dahl, Michael. *Exclamation Points Say "Wow!"* Word Adventures. North Mankato, Minn.: Picture Window Books, 2019.

Hopkins, Lee Bennett. *A Bunch of Punctuation: Poems*. Honesdale, Penn.: WordSong, 2018.

CRITICAL THINKING QUESTIONS

1. What is a question that you would like an answer to?

2. We ask questions to learn about the world we live in. Name some jobs in which you would have to ask lots of questions.

3. What does a detective do? What kinds of questions would a detective ask?

INTERNET SITES

Use FactHound to find Internet sites related to this book.

Visit *www.facthound.com*

Just type in this code: 9781515838623 and go.

 **Super-cool stuff!** Check out projects, games and lots more at **www.capstonekids.com**

OTHER TITLES IN THE SERIES

Commas Say "Take a Break"
Exclamation Points Say "Wow!"
Periods Say "Stop."

Editor: Shelly Lyons
Designers: Aruna Rangarajan and Hilary Wacholz
Creative Director: Nathan Gassman
Production Specialist: Tori Abraham
The illustrations in this book were created digitally.

Picture Window Books are published by Capstone
1710 Roe Crest Drive,
North Mankato, Minnesota 56003
www.mycapstone.com

Library of Congress Cataloging-in-Publication Data
is available on the Library of Congress website.
ISBN 978-1-5158-3862-3 (library hardcover)
ISBN 978-1-5158-4056-5 (paperback)
ISBN 978-1-5158-3866-1 (eBook PDF)

Summary: Question marks want to know the facts.
They help us ask all sorts of questions. Follow
along and learn all about question marks.

Printed and bound in the USA.
PA49